ON PU

NICK LAIRD

On Purpose

——

faber and faber

First published in 2007
by Faber and Faber Limited
3 Queen Square London WC1N 3AU

Typeset by Faber and Faber Ltd
Printed in England by T. J. International, Padstow, Cornwall
Text printed on FSC accredited material

A CIP record for this book
is available from the British Library

ISBN 978-0-571-23738-8

2 4 6 8 10 9 7 5 3 1

For Andrew and Colm

Although you can do things on purpose,
you do them *by* accident.

PAUL BRIANS, *Common Errors in English Usage*

Among the qualities peculiar to me, according to my
nature, was this: my flesh gave off, somewhat, an odor of
sulphur, incense, and other chemicals. This happened, for the
most part, about my thirtieth year when I suffered with a
serious illness. When I had been restored to health my arms
smelled strongly of sulphur. At that time also, I was afflicted
with an itching of the skin . . . Another extraordinary thing
about me was that when I, free from all cares and with the
help of masters, used to study Ptolemy or Archimedes,
I understood neither of them . . .

GIROLAMO CARDANO, *The Book of My Life*

I believe in demonstrations.

HUBERT BUTLER, *Lament for Archaeology*

Acknowledgements

Thanks to the editors of the following publications, where versions of some of these poems have appeared: *Agni*, *Edinburgh Review*, *London Review of Books*, *Oxfam Calendars*, *Poetry London*, *Poetry Review*, *The Pug Dog Club Bulletin*, *The Stinging Fly* and *Times Literary Supplement*.

Thanks to the Chair of Irish Poetry for a residency at the Tyrone Guthrie Centre in Annaghmakerrig.

Many thanks also to Matthew Hollis, Paul Keegan and Edna Longley.

'Lipstick' – based partly on the diary of Lieutenant Colonel Mervin Willett Gonin, DSO, who was amongst the first British soldiers to arrive at Bergen-Belsen, which was liberated in April 1945.

'The Underwood No. 4' – the words in italics are, I think, a paraphrase of a line of Winston Churchill's.

Contents

ON PURPOSE

Conversation

You can't believe the kind of thing
my kind go on about, and I in turn can't
understand the way your lot continually

shout, and shout each other down, and eat as if
someone's about to lift their plate and smash it.
I'd point out what we talk about we talk about

because we speak in code of what we love.
Here. Where afternoon rain pools in the fields
and windows in the houses facing west turn gold.

A flatbed lorry pulls out of the lane.
The mysteries of planning permission.
How someone got pregnant or buried.

The local TV listings. Bankruptcies.
Failed businesses. Convictions. How someone
put the windows in up at the Parish Hall.

How someone else was nailed to a fence.
How they gutted a man like a suckling pig
and beat him to death with sewer rods.

Number 8

They are drilling down through pack ice
in the coldest place on earth,
and finding signs of life:

residues from beech trees,
fossilized, pulled up from half a mile
below sea level and out of other eras –

the Cretaceous, the Triassic, Deep Time,
the very deepest, the kind
you cannot see except inside

the distance of a microscope. Or sleep.

Odd that he made eight, Evagrius,
favoured adherent of Basil the Great,
counsellor to Nectarius, Evagrius the author

of that first long list of sins,
the original deadly ones,
who had to hide when his affair

with the Prefect's wife
came to light, and who settled,
eventually, in the Nitrian Desert

amongst a brotherhood of monks.

Scientists know something used to grow here
and that it might again
since this is waterland and water is unusual.

Antarctica is also the driest place on earth
and so the greatest risk is fire.
They store extinguishers by beds and doors,

loaded with powder like muskets,
for fire is excitable, can catch and take
like all diseases, including, for these

purposes, sadness, number 8.

Holiday of a Lifetime

Your ex transferred
 a photo
to a jigsaw. Years later,
 underneath a shelf,
you find a centre piece.

Sit at the desk. It's mid-
 November.
Your cigarette, neglected,
 unthreads air
to ash. The study's walls are

strung with hoops of light
 thrown by a glass
of water. The sash window
 faces perfectly
north-west. You checked.

How close will you get?
 Introduce it
as a mood composed of pauses,
 water, glass and light,
the sound of distant

traffic passing and someone
 burning leaves
somewhere, close by,
 smoke shrugging
over fences, hedges,

as if to say that everything is
        temporary,
as if you might have momentarily
        forgotten,
you with ash on the sleeve

of your best blue jumper.
        The jigsaw piece
is also blue, as an eye,
        one of yours,
though what you will do

for the rest of your years
        is to try,
repeatedly, to identify
        that blue as sea,
maybe, or sky.

His Scissors

The Laird concentrating is CJ, the Craigavon
Columbo, our Detective Inspector

now playing snooker: one eye tightly shut
and his chin hovering over the cue

while behind him his brother, my father,
ribs him and does an impression

when he finally takes the shot,
of fish-pouty lips, the tongue darting through.

*

If there is a God for us, his name is Darwin,
who came up with answers to the difficulty

and pointed out the principle of action,
direct action, on the nervous system,

how when people use a pair of scissors
they tend to clench their jaws unconsciously

as if to echo or to mimic
the movements of the fingers.

*

Un poco, un peu, diminutive,
immense, enormous, massive.

If you're alone, just now, at home,
get up and go into the bathroom.

Turn on the light to examine your face
and watch how you say it again, please,

this creed of mimicry and adjective:
slow, quick, quick, slow.

*

And then a system of gestures
(since noises are useless for hunting)

and in the right hemisphere
a cluster of neurons occasioned

companionate sound, emotion
inhabiting guttural utterance

(not, note, recollected in peace or composure):
how the mind began shining with language.

*

You are cutting Christmas wrapping paper
with a flutter of the muscles in your jaw.

The word *scissoring* plays on my tongue.
The OED is somewhere in the crime scene

of my study. *Just one more thing, sir,
I'm having a little difficulty, might there,*

*might there have been a struggle here?
The broken lamp. The books on the floor.*

Statue of an Alderman in Devon

You have to drive five counties
and come over the hill to Salisbury Plain,
pass the cloud-shadow grazing
on hayfields and A-roads and grass,
and decelerate into the very last town
where a sign points to the Ice Factory,
and in front of you is sea.

You have to take the second left
to find yourself, lost, of course,
in a hamlet with one phone box
and a bare stretch where seagulls peck
at the bronze feet of an alderman
who watches, like some soul who outlived,
in the end, everyone he loved.

The Happiness of Banging a Nail In

Pick one suitable for masonry.
Each flat or house should set aside
a room for such a purpose. This one,
as you might have guessed, is mine:
so close the door; until it clicks.

Here, the Great Rift Valley,
consciousness, submits to dusk,
and you can focus on an object
located only in the radius
your arms make: a moth, a tooth,

a hand of cards.
                    At some length
you set the nail against the wall
as if you meant to throw a dart,
and weight the hammer in your palm
to peck the tip into the plaster.

The repose of minor measurements!
Each swing and neat assailing tap
that scatters down the grip and wrist,
the spine, the nervous system, that crashes
on the cilia that line the inner ear;

you may pick up a rhythm here,
as the nail is struck, and shunted through
each quick equivocal withdrawal
from this particular continuum
into the night sky of the party wall.

Mandeville's Kingdom

Of Dog-Headed Men and the Juggernaut
I have spoken, I think, and I mentioned
how I mastered the tongue of the Saracen;
I have talked at some length and in detail
of the Head of the Devil in the Vale
Perilous, of Babylon the Less, the Great,

of travelling through the Seven Climates;
I have outlined the lands of Prester John,
the Marvels of Africa, Customs of Canton,
told you of Patmos, Palestine, Pykardy –
but of Paradise, I cannot speak properly,
for I have not been; and that I regret.

What I have always heard from the good
and the wise authorities is
that a wall encircles Paradise,
grown over with moss and yellow bracken
so that no stone is seen, nor anything
from which a wall is made. That barricade

from east to west stretches without entrance;
though the rivers of this world still rise
in the spring that wells in Paradise,
all flow so fast, are treacherous,
ply currents under currents, rocks,
such waves no boat prevails against . . .

You should realize now no living man
can get there. Many great lords tried
at times to forge a course inside,

piloting the waterways to Paradise,
but could not prosper; none survived.
Some died from rowing and exhaustion.

Some went blind and deaf and mad,
the sounds of water were so monstrous.
Others drowned in violence. By chance
I travelled close, once, to Paradise
and at a fording saw such sacrifice:
the bloat dead, face up, discarded.

We journeyed on for ten days south
and passed a snowbound spring
in the palace of a mandarin.
His nails had grown so overlong
he sat all day at table, touching nothing.
They cut his meat for him and placed it in his mouth.

Scouts

Were they Herefords or Lincoln Reds
that followed to the water's edge,
and started when we stopped and sat
to unpack sandwiches and eat?

Someone had dumped a fridge in the stream:
upright, white, so bright it might have been
the doorway to a fifth dimension.

David, who ten years later left
for Orléans to make fighter jets,
slipped off his black Reeboks and socks

but that Christmas past the barracks,
opposite the school, had got a tin
of biscuits packed with Semtex,
and we voted to load up, and walked on.

The Present Writer

Your patience you were taught by the elect, before you left.

Years late you caught the 52 and floated north and free
beneath the Westway out of Ladbroke Grove
passing duvets framed and scumbled by the bedroom windows,

the plaster casts of pillows, and lamp posts ticking past
like the edge of film cells, before this clammy brush
of glossy leaves against the glass two inches from your nose.

The skyline opens up beyond the slowest river
to the gasworks' storage tower
arising like an iron lung or like a real one.

You will do the next thing and the next
and recognize with bleak amusement
each morning as another lost.

A poster on a billboard is being pasted up.
You must be capable and learn to love the place.
Advertisements cannot be the last things singing praises

and you have nothing to sell but the earth itself.
The fraudulent taught you the power of prayer,
or of a form of prayer. Concentration is a form of prayer,

and patience, also.

Everyman

Thou comest when I had thee least in mind.

The hellmouth, to begin with,
three fathom of cord and a windlass,
a link to fire the tinder.

An earthquake: barrel for the same –
we gathered stones the size of fists each time
and rolled them round in it.

Also, a pageant, that is to say,
a house of wainscot,
painted and builded on a cart with four wheels.

A square top to set over said house.
One griffon, gilt,
with a fane to set on said top.

*

Heaven, England, and Hell:
the three worlds we painted as backdrops,
when we left Norwich,

that winter so cold
the rivers slowed to silver roads,
and the oxen thinned to bone.

A rib coloured red.
Two coats and a pair hosen for Eve, stained.
A coat and hosen for Adam, stained.

A face and hair for the Father.
Two hairs for Adam and Eve.
Two pair of gallows. Four scourges. A pillar.

The Year of Our Lord I started the record
for the Coventry Drapers Company
was fifteen hundred and thirty-eight.

Autumns, we'd burn leaves
in cauldrons. In summer
straw would serve, or bark.

If the fire didn't take,
a monstrous Dragon's Mouth
would counterfeit the way below.

Come the new moon from the velvet bag
I drew one shilling five for Thomas and wife,
and six pence for Luke Brown, playing God.

*

The Castle of Perseverance.
Abraham and Isaac.
The Judgement. Noah's Flood.

Each mechanical effect
brought bleats of sudden wonder,
the windlass to lower, the barrel to roll,

the link to set light to the tinder,
although no sound was quite the sound –
that catch of breath caught by the crowd –

when Knowledge, Beauty, Good Deeds,
would take their exit left
and from the right, wordlessly, came Death.

Hunting is a Holy Occupation

To such a length have I gone in loathing
I watched filth building on my skin
and it drop off like the blackened moss
moulting from the cedar tree
when new rains had fattened it heavy.

To such degrees of scrupulosity
my footsteps seemed attended by
a mindfulness that woke a kindness
for the smallest earthly creatures.
I shared their loss and local fear

and sought such forest-solitude
that the whistle of cutter or neatherd
on the forage for wood or edible roots
made me dart like a startled forktail
and when cornered turn rock-still.

In the strict fulfilment of my vows
I learned to couch alone, un-housed,
on river-grit or thorns or flints
and ten unblinking moons I squatted,
moving only a-squat like a toad.

To keep the sacred word revered
I plucked the hair out of my beard,
wore cerements and held my breath
to make the dead give answers:
I was beaten awake with banyan branches,

and survived on the grain of millet and paddy,
snippets of hide and water algae,
on ash and ox-dung, on the cloud-scum
from boiled rice, on the red powder
around the bare husk, on spilt flour.

I never touched spirits.
I never touched flesh. To such a pitch
I've come alone and naked, aching,
licking my hands after eating, waiting,
to learn if God exists, I hate him.

The Search Engine

what is biblical narrative,
pictures form the Bahamas,
things that happened in the 1990s,

off-roading magazines, adult friend finder,
brocciflower dish,
you were gone forever,

Chomsky versus Saussure,
heating with corn,
how mask the aroma of marijuana?

boys bedding, my leg hurts,
small animal habitats,
pictures of Auschwitz, chivalry,

The Alvin Ailey Dance,
how big will aubergines get?
felix vicious, reach out in the darkness,

history of Powerade,
access mobile phone memory,
greatest black asses,

circuit city, the string theory, blizzards

The Immigration Form

Are you now or have you ever been
skilled with silkworm gut or boric lint?
How intimate are you with breathing

through a Carbolic Chinese Twist? Using
the four-hand lift or bamboo splints?
Are you now or have you ever been

conversant, properly, with pain?
Bandages, assorted. Tincture Eucalyptus.
How intimate are you with breathing

through artificial respiration?
There is no time to get assistance.
Are you now or have you ever been

in want of courage or direction?
Cut the body down at once:
how intimate are you with breathing

life into *cadere*, the Latin swoon
beyond cadaver and the cadence?
Are you now or have you ever been?

How intimate are you with breathing?

Pug

Bruiser, batface, baby bear,
bounce in your moon suit
of apricot fur with some fluff
in your mouth or a twig or a feather.

Emperors bored you.

You with the prize-winning ears,
who grew from a glove
to a moccasin slipper
and have taken to secrecy

recently, worming in
under the furniture.
To discover you here
is to keep still and listen.

The settee begins wheezing.

*

Hogarth loved the fact
that for your first half-year
you hardly differed from a rabbit.
When you're over-excited

you tend to get hiccups.

You squeak when you yawn
and your tongue is unfurled
in a semi-circle, salmon-pink
on coastal rock, that trilobite

embedded in the slate
roof of your open mouth,
perfect for the mascot
of the House of Orange.

Your weapon of choice is the sneeze.

*

Above the winter garden
a hair-thin moon, reflecting.
You are open as a haiku,
all *karumi*, hint and sigh.

The Buddha would've liked you.

Watch us from your separate dream
then pad across to clamber through
the plastic flap and plant your paws
four-square again on grass, like this.

Your hackles bristle and you ridge
your back and bark and bark and bark,
at shadows and the fence,
at everything behind the fence,

the cuttings and the railway foxes.

Dissent

And what I assume you shall assume . . .

When he stands behind the podium
you aren't a pixel in the crowd.
If he bangs his fist and drum
your hands don't imitate some bird
trapped in a slick, a storm petrel
that beats, that doesn't know it's beaten.

You will not come to his assistance
or attention. Your face won't loom
out from the stills, an interested moon,
if they ever sift the evidence.
When he comes to put the call in,
when he rings the final tocsin,

when he cries blue ruin and alarum,
be hereabouts or somewhere, talking,
reading a book over dinner,
returning laden from the store.
Don't add to his reckoning:
death is the wages of war,

not sin, and there's no anthem for
the country of your origin,
that landscape you're really in:
the fathomless interior,
the darkest heart no Mungo Park
or Christiaan Barnard tried to chart.

The native guide to lead you through
the blankness on this map is you.
Your truest borders are your skin.
You are your own first citizen,
your plumber and historian,
your chaperone, your one sun-king.

But if by chance you *both* appear
at that age-dark revolving door,
its panelled glass and ambience
suggestive of the Strand entrance
to the Savoy Hotel, that is,
at the gates to heaven, insist

on stepping right into his path
and asking for an autograph:
then as he takes the pen to write
make some remark on grace and doubt,
and the duties of the infidel,
as you pull a can of petrol

from your barrage of shopping bags.

The Garden

*I thought, on the train, how utterly we have
forsaken the earth . . .*
WALLACE STEVENS

All species have evolved to make
themselves competitive in stake
and here is claim and counter-claim –
each leaf a winning paddle raised
at lots of auctioned light, each blade
alert and bidding for the same
thinning, wintry light. Near silent,
just the swish of morning traffic.

You've woken up and wandered down
to watch the garden with the dawn.
The trees are done, tattered nets strung
between the upright poles of trunks.
On next door's newly tar-pitched roof
two pigeons pacify and coo
that if the world draws to a close
the day will be as blank as this,

as overcast, as median
a north-west London morning when
woodsmoke vaults across the fences,
a bluetit's antic in the grass,
and then, elsewhere, white light, a sigh.
As someone drafts an elegy
a vapour trail above zips shut
the body bag of sky. Cheer up.

Your patch has eleven Buddhas
thinking, under separate trees.
The large enlightened limestone one,
beneath the sycamore, has grown
a moss hairdo and mould moustache,
but you, friend, have a train to catch.
You dress and leave. Then board and watch.
Allotments. Flatlands. Building sites.

The satellite commuter towns
grow firebroken, mute, all sound
resurfacing quite suddenly
as another Intercity
eclipses you by inches: flinch
and when it clears, two fat men sit
by the lip of a man-made lake,
their rods perfectly still, and wait.

Like something from Marcel Duchamp,
a gift (with taps) of this white bath
in a field of milking Friesians –
like so many jigsaw pieces
spilled out on green as green as baize.
Around a pylon three sheep graze.
A pale copse of birches jostle,
pale as human skin. Newcastle.

You meant to break the journey
with a pastry and a coffee
somewhere halfway up like York
but nodded off, and woke in dark.
At first you couldn't quite work out
if it was tunnel or the night.
But it was night. You'd no idea
just whereabouts on earth you were.

After the endless fields and towns,
the cellular devastation,
you're suddenly close to the sky –
old snowfall, mountainous country –
before the drift of stars gives way
to trellised glass. One last delay,
The Great North Eastern slides into
the scabbard of the platform. You,

friend, are really me, and hunger
induces us to see those stars
as metaphors, as something else,
as if they *meant* their graceful trawls
of outer space . . . The hour is late.
Each passenger should now alight
and trail their suitcases behind
like little shadows, fat with sins.

The Present Writer

A kitchen moon. The ocean night.
By the sink the purest thing

that I can think is sitting:
like the ghost of a lighthouse

in Atlantic mist,
a full glass of skimmed milk.

*

The wind outside is tugging
at the rigging of clematis

and the filled mast of the apple tree.
We are in bed, two by two,

and side by side as animals.
Bowsprit. Topcastle.

*

Love, I'd turn for you clean-living,
relinquish drinking, fighting, singing.

The ghost can only long in man.
You were asleep but talking.

Which way to the good?
At the next wet, we sail forth.

Light Pollution

You're the patron saint of elsewhere,
jet-lagged and drinking apple juice,
eyeing, from the sixth-floor window,
a kidney-shaped swimming pool
the very shade of Hockney blue.

I know the left-hand view of life,
I think, and it's as if I have, of late,
forgotten something in the night –
I wake alone and freezing,
still keeping to my side.

Each evening tidal night rolls in
and the atmosphere is granted
a depth of field by satellites,
the hammock moon, aircraft
sinking into Heathrow.

Above the light pollution,
among the drift of stars tonight
there might be other traffic –
migrations of heron and crane,
their spectral skeins convergent

symbols, arrows, weather systems,
white flotillas bearing steadily
towards their summer feeding.
A million flapping sheets!
Who knows how they know?

The aids to navigation might be
memory and landmarks,
or the brightest constellations.
Perhaps some iron in the blood
detects magnetic north.

I wish one carried you some token,
some Post-it note or ticket,
some particular to document
this instant of self-pity –
His Orphic Loneliness, with Dog.

Advances? None miraculous,
though the deadness of the house
will mean your coming home
may seem an anticlimax
somehow, and a trespass.

The Tip

You climbed in at Oxford Circus
and out on Willesden Lane.
Even now you get a kick
from doing it, from hailing.

You note how you adopt
the superhero's posture
and slow the vehicle up
as if your hand shot forth

an electro-subatomic ray
and it drew the taxi in,
stopped the nuclear bomb
and saved the heroine,

now her shopping's done.
The cab indicates you've won.

*

Also histrionic, this,
and a category of thing your class,
the ones at home in camouflage,
find marginally embarrassing

like any act you've only seen
effected in the movies
and thus feel false attempting
for yourself, as if all you could

repeat for good were the gestures
of your father, and him his,

keeping some path walked,
some tiny circuit lit.

But look: the cab pulls up,
the door swings back.

*

You met a cabbie once who claimed
to have a perfect memory.
He said that on the morning
you were born, it rained,

then described
the clothes he'd worn,
what he'd eaten, what he'd done.

You were lugging
legal documents in boxes
from his cab onto the kerb.

He said it was a curse,
the sort of thing, honestly,
he wouldn't wish on anyone,
even his enemy.

*

Inside the cab the driver's back
is far away and higher up,
as if he drove a horse and trap
or you sat behind a magistrate,

to transcribe every argument
and silence of his travels
along the district circuit,

around the same chambers,
the different cases.

The people on the pavement
are all hurry and dissolve.
You draw up to the lights and pause
as the centre slips,
and the sound stops.

Gospel

He found me out the back alone,
watering the vines and whistling,
grateful for the evening cool
and his unexpected visit.

He was trembling, tearful with it,
and wouldn't take a drink or sit,
quoted scripture endlessly,
insisted . . . I was stunned.

Only you can lead them to me.
Only you are worthy.
You will sacrifice the man
who clothes me.

Part of me already knew
I'd die without your glory, lord.

Leaving the Scene of an Accident

Stalagmites of bird-lime
under traffic lights and statues,
the unrumbled railway bridges.

Books obsolesce in lockers.
A stork in April makes a nest
in the second reactor's tower.

Like a deep foundation crack,
a single strand of ivy climbs
the gable of the courthouse.

    *

In the eastern suburbs deer appear.
Brushed by waist-high silver steppe grass
and the lighter strokes of barley stalks,

elegant as one might half-expect
the grazing self to be, except her grace
is one complicit in departure.

At the snap and flutter of a shopping bag
snagged in branches, she will break,
and overtake her shadow in the café window.

    *

A wolf, one afternoon in August,
sauntered through the old town square.
By dawn a score were there,

parading past the main post office,
splashing in the People's Fountain,
drinking from it, basking, snarling.

After the storms of autumn pass
black sturgeon ripple, in their turn,
the perfectly circular cooling ponds.

Lipstick

Like nowhere on God's earth, this nightmare
we'd fought all year to liberate, and then
couldn't rouse the sleepers from. How could there

be an adequate description
of that camp, that passage of our lives,
the abject horror in which my men

and I arrived in April 1945.
The place was picked clean as a chicken run,
and everywhere were corpses: some in piles,

some alone or still in pairs, wherever they had fallen.
I fear it was some time before
one could grow accustomed to the sight of men

literally collapsing as one neared,
and could stop oneself assisting.
One had to get one's mind trained to the idea

that an individual did not count. That was the thing:
one knew five hundred souls a day were dying
and that five hundred souls a day were going

to go on falling dead for weeks, before anything
that we could do would have the least effect.
But it wasn't easy watching, say, a child choking

from diphtheria when one could guess
that an instant tracheotomy
would probably have saved her. Scores were left

to choke and drown in their own vomit,
because they lacked the strength to turn aside
and clear a passage for it.

And also dysentery, they squatted
out like animals, relieved themselves in the open.
I saw a woman washing once, naked,

with some general-issue soap and
watched her taking water from a cistern
in which a baby's body floated.

It was hopeless. The Red Cross came, its British
arm, and shortly after – it might not be connected –
there appeared, from somewhere, boxes of it: lipstick.

This was not what we wanted at all. We were calling for a hundred,
a thousand other things. I was embarrassed, then enraged.
Who had requested this – its name was printed

on the shipment – *Everlasting Rouge*?
Would you believe they thought it was the action of a genius?
The internees, when the news

(as it always did) got out, began beseeching
us for *lippenstift, der lippenstift*. For me at least
it was the darkest ring of something, seeing

how those women lay with no nightdress or sheets
but still that redness on their lips. I saw them
wandering, vampiric, red flecks on their teeth,

or sat alone, clown-like and lost. Awaiting post mortem,
lipstick in her clutch, I remember one dead on a table . . .
Dispatched to England in the autumn

[39]

I found my wife's cosmetics, wrapped them in a parcel
and flung it in the tip; though I still see that shade at times,
on hoardings or the high road, young mums, some skinny girl

who's coloured in the colour of her screams.

The Perfect Host

'I hope you don't suppose those are real tears?'
Tweedledum interrupted . . .

As opposed to those that flow
because an onion is reduced to pieces
or smoke strays from the barbecue,

authentic tears, like these, like yours,
contain much higher rates of manganese,
thought responsible for sadness.

Because you must know by now
that it loves you, your body,
and wants you to stay.

Press

The Leader, The Tillamook Headlight,
The Penn and The Cleveland Plain Dealer,
The Beacon, The Olcester Hudsonite,
The Las Vegas Review and The Gleaner.

100% HUMAN HAIR
declared a sign on Christopher.
We saw a President declare a war
in the TV store in Union Square.

The Oregon Emerald, The Forty-Niner,
The Panther and The Pine Bluff Commercial,
The West Plains Daily Quill, The Kingman Miner,
The Point and The Wichita Eagle.

In Gramercy Park I unfolded the Times –
like a map – and watched a solitary ant,
some glossy type risen from the print,
flee the columns and make for the margins.

The Modesto Bee, The Sulphur Times Democrat,
The Sundial and The Commercial Appeal,
The Old Gold and Black, The Daily Wild Cat,
The St Louis Post and The Tar Heel.

The Kernal, The Idaho Mountain Express,
The Crimson White and The Cowl,
The Press, The Winter Park Manifest,
The Blade and The Woonsocket Call.

Appraisal

Features? Embarrassed by their faeces,
omnivorous and sad, awkward beasts
dependent on their tightly metred breath

to keep on feeding, sleeping, breeding.
Oddly they prohibit eating certain species,
like guinea pigs or golden lemurs,

any kind of creatures who can crease
their hairless faces into wrinkles: amusement,
is it, or the purest, dumbest recognition.

They laugh, yes, and snort, and stifle sneezes,
and though they sport the same thin fleeces
in the southern droughts and northern freezes,

so instinctively aggressive is the genus
that they herd in such a way to leave the weakest
prey to what might find it easiest to eat.

Still, wide-eyed in the darkness they fear it.
Part-rational, part-mammal, part-bastard,
yanked along perpetually on leashes by their genes.

Their minds may shine with language, fine,
but what good's that? Words are just pieces like they are,
poor fuckers, who sit on their own in the small hours,

warming a grievance, talking aloud, articulating
tiny myths of struggle and deliverance.
I think they're appealing. I don't mean as in pleasing.

The No in November

Mademoiselle, you took your time.

I suppose a flush of light
and sudden roughness on the heels
of gyroscopic months afloat

comes as some surprise.
Behold, then, the decades spent
adapting to the habitat,

its moodswings and its lack of rhythm,
each evening's news, the central locking,
on how things might appear, at best.

*

Last Saturday we scattered
my wife's father's ashes
in the park behind the Heath,

where I'll take you some day soon
to see the black-necked swans
and ducklings, fluffballs huddled

nervously among the bladed reeds.
It was raining, and since the brim
of the umbrella impinged on all

horizons, the day lacked sky.

*

[44]

When I lifted you out of your sleep,
you were remarkably light:
and in turn Harvey's urn –

plastic, maroon – felt to me
unexpectedly heavy.
Even the ashes were startling,

so kibbled and gritty and white
that afterwards, below the bridge,
the Milky Way lay on the riverbed

in its own calciferous light.

for DMS and HAS

The Underwood No. 4

Grand-piano-black and glossy
    like something Spencer Tracy
played in *Woman of the Year* –
    a real typewriter,

the Underwood, a No. 4,
    invented in 1927
by Franz Augustus Wagner,
    boasting front-stroke mechanism,

single shift and ribbon inking.
    It was seriously raining,
and the thing had gained a great
    evidential weight,

recalcitrant in heft as stone,
    something dead and centred.
As you might expect
    I struggled.

At some point a lollipop lady
    offered to help.
By the rivers of the bus stop
    I sat down and wept.

I bring you things that have been brought
       to something like completion –
a glass of milk, a nectarine,
       that vase of bashful daffodils,

some first edition, second hand,
       this striped nightshirt from Donegal.
At arm's length, the shared life.
       It's broken, of course, like most symbols,

but dense as an engine, all struts and levers,
       and has travelled from Broadway
to the Kilburn Barnardo's,
       where the monarchy are still

adorning teaspoons and the crockery
       and there are never any takers
for Berryman's *Selected*
       or an Everyman copy of *Gatsby*.

Nick Carraway, in fact, must have sat down
       to some machine like this,
but carefully, respectfully, as if to dine
       with relatives and elders.

3

Listen. If tonight a hurricane
          should rip the roof right off,
these walls spin out like playing cards
          across the tracks and baying dark,

the bedclothes whipped like flags
          to kites, the sky straw-flecked
and lightning-spliced and next . . .
          Nothing. Water ticking.

White dawn and patterned birdsong.
          An aftermath dismantling
silence, lobbing words like bricks,
          unearthing this –

a shatter-proof machine,
          its metallic *dang an sich*
persistent in the concrete dust,
          keys filigreed with splinters,

china shards, jags of glass . . .
          Not strength, in the end,
or even intelligence,
          effort, continuous effort.

4

Cars swished past like hovercraft.
        The rain came down in stair-rods
on the single other vertical abroad,
        me, see-thru, now washed,

lugging this incus, this hellmouth
        back home. Dried off,
we lowered it in to the hearth
        like a keystone, exactly.

I wish you what you most want:
        the steady clatter of the stringer
or the foreign correspondent,
        to be never lost for upshot.

Incident. Imagine words flying off
        the red tongue of its ribbon –
and how its weight that afternoon
        took flight, when soaking wet

with rain and sweat, I turned the corner
        of the street and saw
its opposite, an ambulance,
        outside our own front door.

from The Art of War

Over where the pathway goes
through the white magnolias
the charcoal souls of fireflies
are blown on, seriatim.

A mist of stars is drifting in
through the ghost mosquito net,
and the cosmic pulse of crickets
seems inflected, like a question,

now we've got forgiveness down,
are safe and sounded, intricate,
now that even death must count
as treachery, abandonment.

Estimates

Who knows what you mean by love?
Extrapolating from the facts
you want two hundred friends
to watch
you wear the white and walk the aisle.

We could pack the car and motor north
to waterfall and rock, a nightfall
lit by moonlight on the snowfall
patches
still intact among the sheep-tracks

and the turf-banks and the heather.
We could pull in somewhere there,
kill the engine, wait,
listen
to a late-night country music station,

split bars of dark and fruit-&-nut,
sip amaretto from the lid, skin up,
and wake,
unwashed and cramped
as man and wife

in a place unpeopled, dawn-calm,
cleared of its gestures, its features
by weather, to mountains,
and mountains of clouds.
We could.

Waging War

This evening at dinner your very existence
was enough to disprove Darwin.
I outhitlered Hitler.

These nightly show-trials are
becoming tiresome and fractious,
each decree absolute and absurdly revanchist.

You swear that it's me who's obsessed with war,
the sting of a nettle, a national recession,
monsoons and ice avalanches,

and any particular
type of fucking depression
that I might, even now, dare to mention.

Offensive Strategy

Lately the tablets are making no difference.
I have started to cry during adverts again,
and dogs in particular set me off like a drain.

When I get into a fight queuing for petrol
you lie to your friends to account for my temper
and make me ring up for another appointment.

You want me to get a second opinion,
though you put it all down to my father,
just as my mother puts it all down to his.

Another way I can tell it is all going wrong
is I can't get enough nicotine in my system
and nothing will force me to speak.

I run for an hour and still can't get to sleep.
I seem to spend most of my time starting books
and then putting them back on the shelf.

Also, since punching the wall of the study
last Thursday I've been waking each dawn
with a fatter man's hand at the end of my wrist.

It is swollen and red and doesn't quite bend
while my fingers are stiff and insist on remaining
gestured away from the body, as if in disgust.

Terrain

Though we cannot detect them, infra-red rays from the system's
security sensors are scanning the rooms, and our surnames
are secret and neat in security ink on the back of the picture frames,

though readily fluorescent under ultraviolet light. In our own
    rainbow
of visibility, you'd been watching a property show and had dozed,
and now the screen was frantic, driving home through snow, alone.

I read somewhere one-hundredth of that static is cosmic radiation,
interfering from the very edge of space and time, some ninety
    billion
trillion miles away, from the word go, from the Big Bang.

Proponents of string theory posit twenty-six dimensions,
though we have the ability to pick up only four, with these senses
I can now detune – settled in beside your skin and warmth and
    sleep –

to some unnumbered octave, some unremembered reach,
where all the other universes press like lovers up against us.

Attack by Fire

You read it first but I loved it best,
feeling in fact that the effortful voice
of an indulgent obsessive survivor
was something you just wouldn't get,
unaware what it was to grow up
anywhere, even here, and want love.

Slaughterhouse Five gave me to believe
that what can't be seen from this choice
or that can be watched from above –
a Lancaster, say, circling slowly over
something like the surface of the moon,
which reminds his character again of Dresden,

after the phosphorus bombs and the firestorms,
how each scene becomes its own diagram of harm.

Posture of Army

The real thing is camouflage.
Make each gesture
just ambiguous enough
to be taken as offensive.

He who claims quick umbrage
shows himself as foe.
I sketched our crest
and family motto:

ENEMIES DEFINE YOU
BETTER
THAN YOUR FRIENDS

and drew below
the arching print
two pugs belly-up,
pawing mid-air.

You thought I meant
the opposite,
had changed the words
by accident.

Manoeuvring

Manoeuvre, of course, from the Gaelic,
man meaning animal, and *oeuvre* meaning works,
thus *the workings of the beast* –

I heard the bomb at Teebane in which a friend died
and in Brixton once, fucking someone else,
a car backfired unexpectedly and I began to sob.

I couldn't stop. Reader, I almost married *her*.
Soldiers used to whisper beneath my bedroom window
and from the good room once I watched a murderer

get chased across the field beyond the fence,
and saw him punch and swear
and chew the ear off a detective sergeant.

That policeman sat two pews in front
in Derryloran church and knew I stared.
I couldn't stop. You are banging the door

and shouting about leaving.
Someone somewhere told me something,
that kindness is the thing.

Variation in Tactics

I'd laid the emphasis on something else before,
and taken reassurance from the tremor

set in motion by my temper,
content with aught but disregard.

Like every young boy with a difficult father
I demanded a transparent parity.

But it does not have to be so tough.
I do not have to think that he

who looks askance across the restaurant
needs me to fix him with a glance

and I should not feel triumphant
at his embarrassment or fear.

It does not have to be so hard.
I do not always have to shout

or see the last man standing shot
nor walk so fast or coax each little

smithereen or shard of thought
to breaking light, the long-drawn-out,

and lodge it like a toothpick
between my fanged front teeth.

Void and Actuality

The campaign intensifies.
Pete's chosen the wines.
I think this is going over the top,
spending each waking hour

choosing shoes for the church
or cold-calling photographers –
but you have the brownest eyes,
and the irises of mine are blue.

I keep the appointment
where I peel back my sleeve
to display my sore claw
on the cool bed of glass.

And I am aware of being alone
when she steps outside the room
to let the X-ray take and waits
behind the door. Minutes pass

before she frames a storm-sky
in a box of light and smiles.
To undress a doctor!
Her eyes are very green.

She taps the screen to indicate
a break in the clouds of bone.   *There.*
A bright band has forged a weir
through the river of my finger.

It looks like a ring, she said.

The Nine Varieties of Ground

A wheaten sun. The letterbox flicks out its tongue and envelopes
swoon from the door onto the polished oak floorboards,

this swatch of our patchwork terrazzo, our *terra sigillata*.
The sun is different elsewhere – on herringbone parquet in Warsaw,

off *Ulica Bonifraterska,* on cool tiles underfoot in a hotel en-suite
on the thirty-third floor of Toronto, the gummy grey carpet

of your very first study, raked gravel, hot tarmac,
the matted white rug of the Harvard apartment,

a stretch of wet compacted strand in Donegal, the warm mosaic
    of pebbles
in the courtyard of the Captain's House on Lindos,

hard-boiled eggs, you said, from every bird that's ever been.
All that, and all this afternoon a pour of sun

that stirs the hallway floor to yolks and shallow golds,
that folds its light and heat into the lengths of solid oak,

good husbandry as seen from thirty thousand feet.
I mean the edges of the boards are hedges, as from a window seat,

and the boards themselves are tended fields,
some dark with stubble, some lit like wheat.

Use of Spies

Upright and sleepless,
having watched three bad movies,
I am flying across the ocean to see you.

I am a warrior and nothing will stop me,
although in the event both passport control
and a stoned cabbie from Haiti will give it a go,

but I meant to mention something else.

Just before dinner I woke in mid-air,
opened the shutter and saw the sun rising.
Light swung over the clouds like a boom.

The way it broke continually from blue
to white was beautiful, like some fabled
giant wave that people travel years to catch.

I thought I'll have to try and tell you that.

The Hall of Medium Harmony

In lieu of a Gideon Bible
    the bedside table drawer
has a *Lonely Planet Guide to China*
    and a year-old *Autotrader.*

You skim through the soft-tops, the imports,
    the salvage & breakers,
then pick up the book. Over there
    they are eight hours ahead

so it must be approximately dawn
    in the Forbidden City,
where something might evade the guides
    already at the entrance,

might glide right past the lion-dogs
    on guard, asleep in bronze,
might fire the dew on the golden tiles,
    ignite each phoenix on its ridge.

Light. Nine-thousand nine-hundred
    and ninety-nine rooms
begin to warm under its palm.
    Here, in the book, is a diagram.

There is the Hall of Union and Peace.
    The Hall of Medium Harmony.
The Meridian Gate. The Imperial Library.
    The inner golden bridges.

You fidget. You are, you admit, one of
          the earth's more nervous passengers.
But it's different, this, a reasonable space.
          In the palace of an afternoon

a child-king hiding in the curtain
          listening. For a second apart
from the turn of the thing, for a second
          forgetting the narrative's forfeit –

how nothing can outlast its loss,
          that solace is found, if at all,
in the silence that follows each footstep
          let fall on the black lacquer floor

of the now, of the here, where you are,
          in the sunlight, blinking, abroad.